Crushing Candy Crush
for Geniuses

By Carpal T. Syndrome

www.justforgeniuses.com

DISCLAIMER: The book is a work of parody. Nothing in this book is meant to imply any facts about any actual persons or entities.

All rights reserved. No part of this publication may be reproduced, distributed, or transmitted in any form or by any means, including photocopying, recording, or other electronic or mechanical methods, without the prior written permission of the publisher.

Copyright © 2014 by Westlake Gavin Publishers LLC

Just for Geniuses, For Geniuses, and accompanying logos are trademarks of Westlake Gavin Publishers LLC and may not be used without written permission. Candy Crush is a trademark of King.com Ltd or related entities and is not associated with Westlake Gavin Publishers LLC.

HELLO TECH COLLECTION   TGGT1002

Library of *Con*-gress Cataloging-in-Publication Data

Crushing Candy Crush for Geniuses / by Carpal T. Syndrome
p. cm.
ISBN 978-1-63231-993-7
1. Syndrome, Carpal T. 2. Parody, imitations, etc. I. Title.

First Edition

10 9 8 7 6 5 4 3 2 1

Inside...

Sugar Crush every level with the fewest moves and highest score.

Leave your friends behind in a cloud of candy dust.

Combine candies in ways that you never thought possible.

Never have to look at another Lollipop Hammer, Color Bomb, Jelly Fish, or Coconut Wheel ever again.

Stop stealing from your children's college fund to feed your Candy Crush addiction.

Start forming lasting friendships again (instead of friendships predicated on how many free lives you can get...)

And so much more...

Crushing Candy Crush *for Geniuses*

1. Take candy.
2. Place in bag (optional).
3. Crush with hammer.

Crushing Candy Crush *for Geniuses*

Crushing Candy Crush *for Geniuses*

1. Take candy.
2. Place in bag (optional).
3. Crush with hammer.

Read enough? Turn to page 104

Crushing Candy Crush *for Geniuses*

Crushing Candy Crush *for Geniuses*

1. Take candy.
2. Place in bag (optional).
3. Crush with hammer.

Read enough? Turn to page 104

Crushing Candy Crush *for Geniuses*

1. Take candy.
2. Place in bag (optional).
3. Crush with hammer.

Read enough? Turn to page 104

Crushing Candy Crush *for Geniuses*

1. Take candy.
2. Place in bag (optional).
3. Crush with hammer.

Read enough? Turn to page 104

Crushing Candy Crush *for Geniuses*

Crushing Candy Crush *for Geniuses*

1. Take candy.
2. Place in bag (optional).
3. Crush with hammer.

Read enough? Turn to page 104

Crushing Candy Crush *for Geniuses*

1. Take candy.
2. Place in bag (optional).
3. Crush with hammer.

Read enough? Turn to page 104

Crushing Candy Crush *for Geniuses*

1. Take candy.
2. Place in bag (optional).
3. Crush with hammer.

Read enough? Turn to page 104

Crushing Candy Crush *for Geniuses*

1. Take candy.
2. Place in bag (optional).
3. Crush with hammer.

Read enough? Turn to page 104

Crushing Candy Crush *for Geniuses*

1. Take candy.
2. Place in bag (optional).
3. Crush with hammer.

Read enough? Turn to page 104

Crushing Candy Crush *for Geniuses*

1. Take candy.
2. Place in bag (optional).
3. Crush with hammer.

Read enough? Turn to page 104

Crushing Candy Crush *for Geniuses*

1. Take candy.
2. Place in bag (optional).
3. Crush with hammer.

Read enough? Turn to page 104

Crushing Candy Crush *for Geniuses*

1. Take candy.
2. Place in bag (optional).
3. Crush with hammer.

Read enough? Turn to page 104

Crushing Candy Crush *for Geniuses*

1. Take candy.
2. Place in bag (optional).
3. Crush with hammer.

Read enough? Turn to page 104

Crushing Candy Crush *for Geniuses*

1. Take candy.
2. Place in bag (optional).
3. Crush with hammer.

Read enough? Turn to page 104

Crushing Candy Crush *for Geniuses*

1. Take candy.
2. Place in bag (optional).
3. Crush with hammer.

Read enough? Turn to page 104

1. Take candy.
2. Place in bag (optional).
3. Crush with hammer.

Read enough? Turn to page 104

Crushing Candy Crush *for Geniuses*

1. Take candy.
2. Place in bag (optional).
3. Crush with hammer.

Read enough? Turn to page 104

Crushing Candy Crush *for Geniuses*

Crushing Candy Crush *for Geniuses*

1. Take candy.
2. Place in bag (optional).
3. Crush with hammer.

Read enough? Turn to page 104

Crushing Candy Crush *for Geniuses*

1. Take candy.
2. Place in bag (optional).
3. Crush with hammer.

Read enough? Turn to page 104

Crushing Candy Crush *for Geniuses*

1. Take candy.
2. Place in bag (optional).
3. Crush with hammer.

Read enough? Turn to page 104

Crushing Candy Crush *for Geniuses*

1. Take candy.
2. Place in bag (optional).
3. Crush with hammer.

Read enough? Turn to page 104

Crushing Candy Crush *for Geniuses*

1. Take candy.
2. Place in bag (optional).
3. Crush with hammer.

Read enough? Turn to page 104

Crushing Candy Crush *for Geniuses*

Crushing Candy Crush *for Geniuses*

1. Take candy.
2. Place in bag (optional).
3. Crush with hammer.

Read enough? Turn to page 104

Crushing Candy Crush *for Geniuses*

1. Take candy.
2. Place in bag (optional).
3. Crush with hammer.

Read enough? Turn to page 104

1. Take candy.
2. Place in bag (optional).
3. Crush with hammer.

Read enough? Turn to page 104

Crushing Candy Crush *for Geniuses*

Crushing Candy Crush *for Geniuses*

1. Take candy.
2. Place in bag (optional).
3. Crush with hammer.

Read enough? Turn to page 104

Crushing Candy Crush *for Geniuses*

Crushing Candy Crush *for Geniuses*

1. Take candy.
2. Place in bag (optional).
3. Crush with hammer.

Read enough? Turn to page 104

Crushing Candy Crush *for Geniuses*

1. Take candy.
2. Place in bag (optional).
3. Crush with hammer.

Read enough? Turn to page 104

Crushing Candy Crush *for Geniuses*

Crushing Candy Crush *for Geniuses*

1. Take candy.
2. Place in bag (optional).
3. Crush with hammer.

Read enough? Turn to page 104

1. Take candy.
2. Place in bag (optional).
3. Crush with hammer.

Read enough? Turn to page 104

1. Take candy.
2. Place in bag (optional).
3. Crush with hammer.

Read enough? Turn to page 104

Crushing Candy Crush *for Geniuses*

1. Take candy.
2. Place in bag (optional).
3. Crush with hammer.

Read enough? Turn to page 104

Crushing Candy Crush *for Geniuses*

Crushing Candy Crush *for Geniuses*

1. Take candy.
2. Place in bag (optional).
3. Crush with hammer.

Read enough? Turn to page 104

Crushing Candy Crush *for Geniuses*

1. Take candy.
2. Place in bag (optional).
3. Crush with hammer.

Read enough? Turn to page 104

Crushing Candy Crush *for Geniuses*

Crushing Candy Crush *for Geniuses*

1. Take candy.
2. Place in bag (optional).
3. Crush with hammer.

Read enough? Turn to page 104

Crushing Candy Crush *for Geniuses*

Crushing Candy Crush *for Geniuses*

1. Take candy.
2. Place in bag (optional).
3. Crush with hammer.

Read enough? Turn to page 104

Crushing Candy Crush *for Geniuses*

Crushing Candy Crush *for Geniuses*

1. Take candy.
2. Place in bag (optional).
3. Crush with hammer.

Read enough? Turn to page 104

Crushing Candy Crush *for Geniuses*

1. Take candy.
2. Place in bag (optional).
3. Crush with hammer.

Read enough? Turn to page 104

1. Take candy.
2. Place in bag (optional).
3. Crush with hammer.

Read enough? Turn to page 104

1. Take candy.
2. Place in bag (optional).
3. Crush with hammer.

Read enough? Turn to page 104

Crushing Candy Crush *for Geniuses*

Crushing Candy Crush *for Geniuses*

1. Take candy.
2. Place in bag (optional).
3. Crush with hammer.

Read enough? Turn to page 104

Crushing Candy Crush *for Geniuses*

Crushing Candy Crush *for Geniuses*

1. Take candy.
2. Place in bag (optional).
3. Crush with hammer.

Read enough? Turn to page 104

Crushing Candy Crush *for Geniuses*

1. Take candy.
2. Place in bag (optional).
3. Crush with hammer.

Read enough? Turn to page 104

Crushing Candy Crush *for Geniuses*

1. Take candy.
2. Place in bag (optional).
3. Crush with hammer.

Read enough? Turn to page 104

Crushing Candy Crush *for Geniuses*

1. Take candy.
2. Place in bag (optional).
3. Crush with hammer.

Read enough? Turn to page 104

Crushing Candy Crush *for Geniuses*

Crushing Candy Crush *for Geniuses*

1. Take candy.
2. Place in bag (optional).
3. Crush with hammer.

Read enough? Turn to page 104

Crushing Candy Crush *for Geniuses*

1. Take candy.
2. Place in bag (optional).
3. Crush with hammer.

Read enough? Turn to page 104

1. Take candy.
2. Place in bag (optional).
3. Crush with hammer.

Read enough? Turn to page 104

Crushing Candy Crush *for Geniuses*

Crushing Candy Crush *for Geniuses*

1. Take candy.
2. Place in bag (optional).
3. Crush with hammer.

Read enough? Turn to page 104

Yep, that's it. That's the whole book.

We know that Candy Crush fans enjoy repetition but, honestly, how many more times do we need to repeat it? If fifty times is not enough, we suggest you read the book again. As many times as it takes.

You got the point right away? That's wonderful news, but not surprising. After all… you are a Genius!

 Use it as a notebook. (The left sided pages have been lined for your convenience.)

 "Gift it forward" Give the book to an unsuspecting friend, family member, or colleague—and help upset even more Candy Crush fans. Try it. It's fun.

 Add it to your *Just for Geniuses*™ collection. No promises, but serious collectors are expecting the value of all *Just for Geniuses*™ branded merchandise to substantially rise in the decades and centuries ahead.

Nonetheless, we would like to thank you for taking precious time away from playing Candy Crush to read this book.

We couldn't write books like this without readers like you to support us. Any feedback you give would be greatly appreciated. We have fragile egos, so be gentle about it. Or funny.

Please give us feedback at
www.justforgeniuses.com/feedback

Sorry to hear that. But don't despair. The real power of the *Just for Geniuses*™ brand is the flexibility and the ability to customize it **to your needs**. Think gifts, collectibles, promos, charity fund-raising, corporate events, advocacy, and much more.

Depending on your needs, we have the perfect solution for you:

- Submit a customization request to our design team at no cost. (We will try to accommodate everyone's request based on our discretion.)
- Ask our Professional Services team to assist you (minimum order applies.) This is necessary for time-sensitive requests.
- License *Just for Geniuses*™ for your product, service, or media needs. This would give you the most flexibility.

What are you waiting for? Submit your request today at **www.justforgeniuses.com/solutions**

Crushing Candy Crush *for Geniuses*

www.justforgeniuses.com

www.ingramcontent.com/pod-product-compliance
Lightning Source LLC
Chambersburg PA
CBHW070854050426
42453CB00012B/2187